The Ontario Tradition in York County

MENNONITE FURNITURE

Lynda Musson Nykor and Patricia D. Musson

Foreword by Nancy-Lou Patterson   Photographs by Martha Kuehner

James Lorimer & Company, Publishers
Toronto 1977

ISBN 0-88862-148-5   0-88862-149-3
Design: Don Fernley

James Lorimer & Company, Publishers
35 Britain Street
Toronto

Canadian Cataloguing in Publication Data

Musson, Patricia, 1945-
  Mennonite furniture

Bibliography: p.
ISBN 0-88862-148-5 bd. ISBN 0-88862-149-3 pa.

1. Furniture, Mennonite — Ontario. I. Musson Nykor,
Lynda, 1940-   II. Title.

NK2442.06M88   749.2'113   C77-001430-5

Printed and bound in Canada

Contents

Foreword   5

Acknowledgements   8

Introduction   9

1 Dissent and Exodus   11

2 The Journey to Upper Canada   27

3 The Furniture and Its Makers   41

4 The Homes and Meeting Houses   73

Conclusion   89

Notes   91

Bibliography   93

For Robert

"... little and unknown, loved and prized by God alone."
— *The Reesor Family in Canada*

Foreword

Studies of Canadian native and ethnic arts have been appearing in the 1970s with ever greater rapidity, and a whole new generation of specialists is emerging. The movement is, of course, not really new. Significant pioneering efforts appeared early in the century, but the current activity is more intense and is receiving more public attention. One of many such areas of interest in the field of ethnic studies is that of the Germanic communities of southern Ontario. A number of books of greater and lesser scholarship have appeared that allow students, enthusiasts, and *amateurs* a new look at this bright portion of the Canadian mosaic.

The *amateur* is a lover, and those who love the artifacts of other cultures see the passions of other lives shining back at them from the past or present. The artifact becomes a kind of burning glass to focus this contact. Different people read artifacts differently; they find and value different kinds of meaning in them, but all go through a definite process.

First, the objects must be found. That may seem self-evident, but it is an exacting and even exhausting task. Sometimes the job is done by "collectors" who bulldoze their way through the countryside as builders do through a cache of bones, scattering objects right and left, whether into their own pockets or the pockets of others. Genuine destruction, both psychic and physical, can come of such procedures. When I first began my research among the Swiss-German and Dutch-German Mennonite communities of southern Ontario, I was put in touch with the redoubtable Blodwen Davies. In my innocence I said I thought my findings would be of interest to "collectors," and touched off an explosion measurable in megatons! Many years and some bitter as well as much pleasurable experience later, I know why she was so upset.

The task of searching and finding is sometimes done by people who, like Parsifal in the Grail Castle, do not know the right questions to ask. Artifacts alone, without their "origin stories," their backgrounds, histories, and present positions, are less meaningful whatever their aesthetic value. Sometimes, as with this book, there is a combination of industry and tact, of patience and meticulousness, that can find, record, identify, and leave *in situ* the relics of other people's lives. Someday these lovely things ought to go, carefully documented, into public collections, after their personal meanings have rubbed off, after families no longer want to keep them. For now they lie in their ancestral earth, still lovingly attended by their inheritors.

We can thank Lynda Musson Nykor and Patricia Musson and their photographer Martha Kuehner for having perfomed this difficult and delicate task. The images are here. We can study them at our leisure and to our satisfaction, visually at least. Further research will not find the ground disturbed and the relics scattered.

A second task is that of learning what other people have already said about objects like the ones newly found. I detect a vigorous effort to do this; the bibliography reveals an industrious examination of works of the history of furniture and architecture, the history of religion, the history of Mennonites, the history of Canada. There has been a serious attempt to bring them together into a meaningful whole. Probably specialists in each of these areas will find things left out, things less than accurately expressed, but in a generalist work this is inevitable. There is a certain courage in undertaking the task, and in the main it has been done with clarity and a good will. Non-specialists can read the same resource works for themselves, and they will find they have been given good guidance.

The third task is the most delicate of all. It is the process of interpretation. What do these objects mean? What cross-cultural currents do they reveal? What have been their influences? What were the purposes they were intended to fulfill? What can we learn of the lives of the people who made and used these objects from the artifacts themselves? It is here that the writers have been most daring and most interesting. I do not suppose that all their interpretations will be agreed upon by specialists: new evidence, new ideas will keep these matters in motion anyway, but the effort is significant in itself. The writers sat in the kitchens and parlours, examined the old Bibles and family records, drove the country roads and city streets, visited the meeting houses and places of worship, and haunted the museums and collections. Their impressions and intuitions are thus of intense interest, and merit our respect. These are the thoughts of writers who have encountered otherness in a spirit of openness, acceptance and love.

Nancy-Lou Patterson
Associate Professor of Fine Art
University of Waterloo
Waterloo, Ontario

Acknowledgements

This kind of project, in which furniture is examined and photographed in private homes, cannot possibly be done by three individuals alone. It involves the fullest co-operation of many families and furniture-owners. In our case, these were the descendants of Pennsylvania pioneers who came to Upper Canada nearly two centuries ago — the Mennonites, Dunkards and Brethren in Christ who graciously gave us their time and knowledge. Respect for their privacy prevents us from naming them, but they furnished us with a long oral tradition from which we drew much of our information. In many instances family Bibles and fraktur birth and marriage certificates validated chronologies, and wherever possible we attempted to factually document our findings from other sources.

We spent a great deal of time establishing contact with these families and were helped in this by Gwen Allchuch and Reg Good as well as by the ministers of many of the churches, in particular Reverend Paul Martin of the Wideman Mennonite Church in Markham.

Lynn McMurray, John MacIntyre, Peter and Hilary Neary, Alfred LeMesurier, Walter Cooper, Joy Elder, Frank Rodgers, Saralee Turner, Douglas Richardson, Henry Dobson and Valerie Wyatt were but a few of the many others who assisted and advised us in putting this book together. The staffs of the Thornhill Community Centre Library, the Markham Public Library and the Weldon Library at the University of Western Ontario provided us with all of the source material we asked for. We would also like to thank the Ontario Arts Council for their financial assistance.

LN and PM

Introduction

No comprehensive study of the Germanic tradition in Canadian furniture-making has ever been undertaken, and few attempts have been made to distinguish the Germanic style from that of other pioneer groups. This book examines one small but vital facet of that tradition by documenting in words and photographs the furniture made by the Mennonites who settled in York County, Ontario at the end of the eighteenth century.

The pioneer experience was not new to the York County Mennonites. Just over a hundred years before, their ancestors from Switzerland and the German Palatinate had emigrated to America after two centuries of being pursued and persecuted throughout Europe. Their search for religious and social freedom led them to Pennsylvania, where they played a major role in the settlement of the new land.

Mennonite furniture is a map of this eventful past, and to fully appreciate the accomplishments of the York County furniture-makers it is necessary to know something of Mennonite history. The European background that shaped beliefs and customs, the years in America, the events that prompted the move north — all of these factors had an impact on the craft of furniture-making.

When the Mennonites arrived in Upper Canada to settle near Niagara and in Waterloo and York counties, they began to make furniture that both retained the basic Germanic shape and spirit and showed the influence of contact with other cultures, especially the American. The unique characteristics of this furniture arose out of the particular religious convictions of the Mennonites and distinguish it from other furniture of Germanic origins.

Different conditions in the three settlements in Upper Canada produced clearly defined regional variations. Waterloo furniture was similar to that made in Pennsylvania, while Niagara furniture moved away from the American models. In York County, Mennonite furniture made in the two pockets of settlement in Markham and Vaughan townships followed a middle course; it remained firmly enough rooted in the larger German-Ontario tradition to shed valuable light on that area, but at the same time retained its ties to Europe and America. Because of its unusual blend of influences, we have chosen to direct most of our attention to the York County hybrid.

Much of the first permanent furniture made by Mennonites is still in use today, owned and cherished by descendants of the settlers who came to Upper Canada nearly two hundred years ago. Often the furniture is still standing in the same farm homes for which it was built. We feel there is an added dimension to furniture still in its rightful milieu, and, with the exception of a few pieces photographed in the Markham Museum, the pictures on the following pages show the furniture in everyday use.

1 Dissent and Exodus

The Catholic Church dominated medieval Europe. It was the repository of classical knowledge and the centre of all scholarship. Its years of uncontested authority, however, had led it into numerous oppressive practices. It levied exorbitant taxes, sold holy water and indulgences and conscripted armies to extend its sphere of influence. Secular rulers, in turn, passed on these heavy burdens to that luckless class, the peasantry.

But by the end of the fifteenth century, probing, unsettling ideas from a still classically oriented Italy were sweeping into northern Europe. The Renaissance, with its emphasis on humanism and scientific enquiry, created a climate favourable for reformations of various kinds, and before Martin Luther had even formulated the ultimatums he would nail to the cathedral door in Wittenburg, sects considered heretical by the church and rebellious by the state had begun to emerge. Increasingly rampant religious and social strife marked the first quarter of the new century, culminating in 1525 in the Peasants' War. That year also saw the formation of a group in Switzerland that was to spread its doctrines the entire length of the Rhine Valley, into duchies and principalities to the east and west and as far north as the Netherlands.[1] Its members, some of whom believed that radical measures were necessary to change society, some merely seeking to worship in peace according to what they read in Luther's recently-translated vernacular German Bible, were called Anabaptists, "the most separated brethren of the Protestant Reformation."[2]

The Anabaptists preached not only religious separation, but withdrawal from all worldly involvement. They refused to participate in civic affairs and adopted a severely plain style of dress that stressed their apartness. Determined not to be forced into the armies of either prince or pontiff, most became strict pacifists. But their most serious offence concerned baptism, a rite they felt could only be appreciated by the fully mature adult. To both church and state, infant baptism had more than just religious significance; it provided the only sanctioned rite of passage into a society they jointly regulated. Thus when the Anabaptists publicly baptised some of their adult members, they made the supreme gesture of defiance to these twin authorities. Officialdom saw that "the new baptism was an anarchical threat to the maintenance of a united, homogenous and serene society,"[3] and showed its disapproval; the movement was quickly banned, and persecutions and martyrdoms soon followed.

But Anabaptism persisted, and its members proposed a wide variety of solutions to the problems besetting those who sought refuge inside its fold. The initial movement produced a number of splinter groups, many of which espoused similar beliefs and were divided only on the means of practicing them. One of the most prominent of the sects to emerge from Anabaptist roots, and the one that achieved the greatest unity, was the group that organized under the leadership of Menno Simons (1496-1561), a former Dutch priest and a contemporary of John Calvin. The sect took its name from its leader, and members were known as Menists or Mennonites.

Anabaptism, like most successful revolutionary movements, was at first concentrated in the cities, and many of its members were artisans or merchants. In northwestern Germany and Holland Mennonism retained its urban character,[4] and Mennonite artisans were in an ideal position to absorb not only the religious and social ferment of the Renaissance, but also the cultural and artistic richness. They were privy to new developments in all of the arts and especially to new developments in the craft of furniture-making, which they would later share with rural Mennonites in America.

In Switzerland, Austria and southern and central Germany the urban base soon shrunk in importance, while the faith continued to spread and flourish among the rural peasantry. Mennonites in these country areas lived and farmed communally, a way of life that was to play a large part in making them successful pioneers in the new world. Living in such close proximity, they were able to make use of each other's skills, and a degree of specialization, the essential first ingredient in even the most rudimentary of furniture-making traditions, began to develop. Later in America, when the communal way of life which encouraged specialization in rural Europe came into contact with the skills and knowledge of the Mennonites who had urban European roots, a furniture-making tradition of a high order of competence emerged.

Several factors combined to make furniture-making an increasingly important craft in fifteenth-century Europe. With the rebirth of classicism, the landed classes began to express an interest in acquiring things of a decorative and permanent nature for their homes. Exploration and trade with distant parts of the world both gratified and intensified this desire, as did a burgeoning commercialism which brought wealth and power to the cities. These factors gave rise to guilds of a new order — guilds that would further the spread of craftsmanship and promote the fresh concepts in design demanded by a populace recently awakened to the beauties of the material world. Gradually the interest in new designs spread into the countryside, and the peasantry made rough imitations of the useful and attractive objects that were so rapidly gaining in popularity.

As feudal society shifted and changed, the functions of furniture changed, too. The folding stool that had once been a throne for a king or duke acquired arms and a back and became a chair or bench in the house of a yeoman or merchant. The ogee-arched and tracery-embellished chest that had once transported a knight's belongings gained drawers and feet, grew taller and became a desk or cupboard.

As furniture became more and more a necessary component of every home, new developments rapidly improved construction methods and appearance. First, the mortise and tenon joint, a construction technique lost to western Europe for many centuries, was rediscovered and put into use. Next, the development of the frame and panel technique eliminated the need for heavy timbers crudely nailed together or fastened with iron bindings. This innovation meant that furniture could now be constructed of a frame grooved on the inside so that a panel could be slid into it to form a light, solid surface. By the end of the sixteenth century another innovation, the dovetail joint, allowed smooth-cornered drawers to glide easily in and out of furniture cases. Over the next half century the primitive single dovetail gave way to the more refined series of small dovetails.[5]

In addition to these technical innovations, furniture was transformed by distinctive national characteristics. In Holland and Germany proportions remained close to the earth, functional rather than graceful, heavy and somewhat squat. The handsomeness of a piece lay in the exquisitely-wrought embellishment and decoration, the veneer, inlay and marquetry for which the Dutch in particular were becoming famous throughout Europe.

Painting and carving, which had been the favoured means of decoration in early roughly-constructed furniture, continued to be used, partly to enhance rather than hide the new methods of wood construction and partly because old traditions were discarded slowly if at all, especially in rural areas. Country craftsmen often imitated veneer, inlay and marquetry patterns with a paint brush, since these complicated techniques usually proved too difficult for crude tools and untrained hands. Often the painted designs were almost as beautiful and ornate as the ones they imitated. Gradually the floral motifs and geometric shapes of marquetry and inlay combined with religious and naturalistic symbols to form a unique kind of folk art.

It was at this stage of furniture production that the Anabaptist groups began to be dispersed throughout Europe and across the Atlantic to America. At the invitation of Catherine the Great, some of the Dutch and German Mennonites emigrated to Russia, where they lived for many years until official policies on conscription once again brought them into conflict with civil authorities. These Mennonites eventually came to Canada and played a large part in the settling of the prairie provinces.

Many more of the Anabaptists, especially those from Switzerland, where persecutions were to continue until the nineteenth century, and from the German Palatinate, took part in a westward emigration as participants in a "holy experiment." Most chose to settle in Quaker Pennsylvania, both because free land was available and because the religious and social atmosphere was congenial. Like the Anabaptists, the Quakers objected to military service and the swearing of oaths, and the laws of the new colony were designed to protect these beliefs. In 1683 the first community to include Mennonites was established at Germantown and would eventually leave its mark on American history by being the first to register a protest against the practice of slavery.[6] Soon other Anabaptists, including the German Baptists or Dunkards who would later go to York County with the Mennonites, were taking up land in the colony.

The Anabaptists quickly became noted for their productivity on the land. Swiss Mennonites originated the practice of crop rotation and the use of lime and manure to replenish the soil.[7] And Mennonite farmers were the first to consider the structure that housed the livestock of equal importance to the family home. In a short time their sturdy barns dotted the landscape.

The first homes were much like those they had left behind in Europe. But the homely log and stone cabins were soon replaced by large, stone, brick or frame dwellings that testified to the prosperity of the Mennonite farmers.[8]

When farms had been established and homes constructed, furniture was built. In America, as in Europe, Mennonites settled close to one another on adjoining pieces of land.[9] Specialization of skills began to reappear soon after the initial period of land-clearing, and although apprenticeships in the true sense of the word were unknown in the Mennonite farm villages, continuity and competence were assured as furniture-making skills were passed on from generation to generation.

European traditions soon mingled with those already in America and out of this melting pot of design and method came furniture that was distinctive and different from that being made anywhere else. As new styles came to the colonies from Europe, they were modified by the urban cabinet-maker to conform to the tastes of colonial society. The rural furniture-maker or joiner re-interpreted these Americanized versions, often adding some traditional features rather than attempting to make complete copies. Thus furniture made by Mennonite craftsmen showed touches of the colonial William and Mary, Queen Anne and Georgian periods on the heavy rectangular German structures. When Queen Anne furniture came to the colonies, for example, the carved shell or fan motif that graced the chests of drawers and highboys was taken up and carved on many country pieces, but the cabriole legs of the style usually had to be rejected because they were difficult to reproduce in soft woods and without precision tools. The finials and arched broken pediments that gave the fine furniture added height and impressiveness were occasionally found on rural pieces, but usually only on the clock cases which were narrow enough to permit a manageable version of the design.

The woods available to rural American furniture-makers often limited the intricacy of their designs. In the cities cabinet-makers with sophisticated tools and years of training were able to work with difficult hard woods such as native walnut and imported mahogany. Some cabinet-makers, such as those who favoured the Chippendale style, used soft woods like pine when the occasion demanded. But the rural craftsman almost always made his furniture from the softer woods, usually white or yellow pine and only occasionally oak or maple. Walnut was seldom used and then only for the most straight-forward pieces. The softness of these woods made finely-carved or delicate pieces of furniture almost impossible to build.

To make up for these limitations, the rural furniture-maker turned to decoration. Paint was used to duplicate the more desirable wood grains and to accentuate particularly interesting grained sections, like the burls that became popular in William and Mary's reign. Two coats of paint would be applied; the first acted as an undercoat and the second was streaked with a comb, sponge or the fingers while still wet to produce the grained effect. If a grain such as bird's-eye maple was wanted, the fingertips were dabbled in the wet paint.

Painted folk art designs were also used to decorate furniture, although at first these were reserved for dower chests. Gradually colourful Swiss and German symbols began to mingle on these pieces with motifs used by pioneers of other nationalities. For example, the tulip used lavishly by the Scandinavians often appeared side by side with Germanic flowers and birds. Soon the Pennsylvania counties developed their own distinctive styles of decoration for boxes and chests: in Lancaster County, for example, these pieces featured painted panelled arches; in Montgomery County furniture-makers favoured geometric designs.[10] Inlay, in small patterns of stars or diamonds, was another popular means of decoration, and veneer was used occasionally on the finest pieces of country furniture.

Methods of construction were passed around in the same way as designs and decorations and were altered in response to new conditions. The elaborate iron bindings found on European chests, for instance, were largely eliminated in America. They had once been used to give portable pieces added strength, but in the permanent homes of America such supports were no longer needed. Iron-bound chests became common again for a short time when the Mennonites began their emigration to Upper Canada, but faded from usage once the pilgrimage was over. New objects such as deed boxes, which became a necessity when the Mennonites for the first time became property-owners, were added to the repertoire of the craftsman. New skills such as stencilling were learned in America, and by the nineteenth century this was a popular decorative flourish on chairs, benches, day beds, table legs, cupboards and even kitchen implements and containers. In the large permanent homes built-in furniture became increasingly popular; built-in corner cupboards replaced or augmented the free-standing *schranke*, and wall-hanging cupboards and cabinets were a common feature of many homes.

Generally Pennsylvania Mennonite furniture had a simplicity that was largely a reflection of the plain tastes of neighbouring Quakers. But if the furniture in the farm homes was a good deal less grand than that found in the homes of wealthy Philadelphians, it was at least carefully wrought, pleasing to the eye and, most of all, plentiful. Before the Mennonites had been in America a century, their neat, spacious homes were filled with an abundance of useful pieces.

A few simple but critical tools determined the shape of country furniture. The lathe, in particular, was used extensively. Lathe-turned chairs, often with the distinctive mushroom finials on the front posts, could be made quickly and easily, as could slat or ladder-back chairs, a strictly American version of the turned chair. Little in the way of upholstered furniture ever found a place in a Mennonite home; most chairs had simple bark, cane or rush seats. Windsor chairs became as popular in rural areas as the ladder-backs, largely because of their simplicity of construction; turned members were slotted into slab seats, eliminating the need for nails or screws.[11]

Tables in colonial America were of three main types. The most common, and the earliest, was the sawbuck table which had a base that resembled a saw-horse. Tables with stretcher bases or plank tops and lathe-turned legs were also common. Plank-topped tables usually had from one to three drawers and occasionally pegged spline tops which could be removed.

Court or press cupboards were an established feature in colonial homes by the time the Mennonites had arrived and begun to build the similar Dutch *kas* and German *schranke*. These massive storage units for food, linens and other household necessities were usually constructed so as to be easily disassembled. Most had the common ball or flattened bun feet, a legacy from Europe, and solid rather than glass-paned doors. Later the linen press, a somewhat lighter but still large piece with solid doors, became popular in many homes. Cupboards or dressers for dishes had simple bracket feet with solid doors and three drawers, a Germanic feature, in the bottom part of the unit. The top sections had glass-paned doors (in cupboards) or open shelves (in dish dressers).

Bureaus or chests of drawers were infrequently used by country people in the early years because most clothing was hung on pegs. In later years, when chests of drawers became common, they were frequently decorated in the same way as dower chests and blanket boxes were. They shared the space in the bedroom with lathe-turned beds that were constructed with pegs so that a rope lacing supported a tick or mattress.

Mennonite furniture-making flourished in Pennsylvania. Dressers for dishes, handsome cupboards, benches, chairs and tables, beds covered with quilts and coverlets, flour bins, dough trays, candle tables, hanging cabinets, spinning wheels and pie and jam cupboards softened the somewhat austere existence of the farm Mennonites.

By 1776, however, the peaceful existence was shattered. War with Britain led to a growing resentment with the Mennonites' pacifism, making life highly uncomfortable and even treacherous for them.[12]

Rights that had been guaranteed when they first came to the colony were revoked by assemblies more sympathetic to the cause of autonomy than to that of pacifism. When the opportunity presented itself, the Mennonites and other non-conformists decided it was time for yet another move into an unknown land.

(Left) The yellow over cream paint-graining of this 1836 pine clock case makes it a spectacular example of early Mennonite craftsmanship. The broken arched pediment indicates the American influence, while the double cornice was a common feature of many Markham Mennonite clock cases.

(Right) Mennonites who settled Maryland near the Pennsylvania border built this clock and later shipped it to Markham, probably by rail. The case is of cherry and has been dated ca. 1750, although the top may have been built later than the bottom. A string which hangs from its side can be pulled to make the clock strike the next hour.

(Top) This ministerial table is still in the Edgeley Mennonite Church, now in Black Creek Pioneer Village. It may be as old as the church which was built in 1824. The squared, tapered legs and single drawer with wooden pull indicate early construction. The table has a pegged spline top that could be easily removed.

Tables with lathe-turned legs and no stretchers were the most common type in York County. This one, ca. 1835, has a pine top of three boards held together by spline joints. The top is held to the bottom by pegs through splines and is removable. The bottom section of the table is of butternut.

Rockers with a step to facilitate the nursing of an infant appear to be unique to Markham. The older one with the full step was made before 1850. The other has an innovative half step which ensured that the heel did not catch when getting up from the chair. This later chair was originally painted red and has more elaborate turnings than are found on most Mennonite chairs in the township. It has been used by at least five generations of the same family.

(Left) Samuel Moyer made this ladder-back rocker in Vineland, though it was found in a Markham home. The walnut arms have unusual bent-wood side supports, and the woven bark seat is the original.

(Right) The original black paint and gold stencil design still grace this fine Markham Mennonite rocker. The arms have typically Germanic construction, with the tenons of the front posts going through the arm and held by wedges. The seat is original.

These two chairs, once part of a set of six, still have the original blue finish and yellow painted decoration. The button terminals on front and back posts indicate the American ancestry, but the unusual shaping of the back slats is a feature so far only found on Markham Mennonite chairs.

(Opposite) Ester Reesor died of consumption in this fine spindle back rocker, and her passing was commemorated in the needlework sampler above it. The chair is black with yellow painted decoration. Although it was found in Markham, the decoration indicates it may have been brought to the township from the Niagara area.

Plain pine benches with a single board back were customary in most York County
Mennonite meeting houses. This one, from the Wideman Church in Markham, is
unusually elaborate, but the shaping of the arms and base is very similar to that found
on Pennsylvania church furniture. At one time it was stained a reddish brown.

2 The Journey to Upper Canada

Thousands of years ago the ice caps that cover the earth's surface spread further out onto the land masses, twisting the terrain, uprooting vegetation and permanently altering the shape of whole continents. In the northern part of Ontario fertile soils were scraped away by this glaciation, and when the icy tide receded, only bare outcroppings and shallow valleys filled with heavy clays were left. In time vast tracts of towering, sky-darkening conifers grew over much of this area. To the south, in the peninsula formed when the ice scooped out the basins for the Great Lakes, the rich soils pushed down from the north came to rest in glacial gulleys and depressions and eventually began to support a widely diverse deciduous forest of beech, maple, oak, basswood, black cherry, ironwood, walnut, poplar, elm, hickory, tulipwood and butternut. In fact so dense was the growth of trees over the whole province that at the turn of the nineteenth century Robert Gourlay in his *Statistical Account of Upper Canada* could still refer to it as "one continuous forest."[1]

Before the American Revolution, few Europeans had settled in this intimidating territory, nor were the Loyalists who left the thirteen colonies to fight on the side of the British Crown given land there. Instead, they were assigned grants in the older part of the territory among the French-speaking inhabitants or in Nova Scotia and New Brunswick.

To the British back home it was a matter of some debate whether the colonial possession north of the Great Lakes and west of the St. Lawrence was worth developing at all. It was thought that, if this area was left entirely to the Indians to whom it legally belonged, the chance of wars with these native allies would be lessened.[2]

But gradually, as refugees from the War of Independence appeared in increasing numbers at border forts such as Niagara, and as Loyalists pressed for land suitable for farming, those in charge of settlement policy began to reconsider their views. They decided that leaving the land along the banks of the St. Lawrence to the French would provide a sufficient barrier to the flow of dangerous republican ideas emanating from English-speaking America, and by 1784 the western part of the territory was opened for settlement. The first permanent settlers, members of the disbanded Butler's Rangers, settled near Niagara, and in 1786 the first small band of Mennonites, five men who had walked all the way from Pennsylvania, joined them in the area. By 1802 there were thirty-three Mennonite families living at Jordan and Vineland on farmland they had purchased (only Loyalists who had actually fought for the British were eligible for free land), and some of their number had begun to move into the Welland area.[3]

The journey into this rugged land was never easy, whether on foot or in the Conestoga wagons developed by the Mennonites for the move to the north. Dr. Frank Epp in his *Mennonites in Canada* describes the journey: "For most of the immigrants, the 400 or more miles covered included the crossing of the Susquehanna, the mighty Niagara, and other great rivers as well as the Allegheny mountains. Some trails could be trod only after they were widened with scythe and axe. Some mountains could be ascended only if the wagons were unloaded and some narrow passes crossed only after the wagons were disassembled. Rivers were bridged with rafts or with floating corduroy hastily put together, or by converting the tightly sealed wagons into boats. Many times the passengers, including women and children, walked for long stretches because the loads were too heavy and the roads too muddy."[4] But come they did, in spite of hardships.

By 1788 the British, growing more and more conscious of the desirability of a vigorous North American empire, came to realize that the decision to allow settlement in the area had been a wise one. Government policy was formulated to further encourage settlement and to control it. Although the conditions for settlement outlined in this policy were frequently misinterpreted, causing widespread land speculation, many settlers were attracted to the area. By 1791, when Quebec was divided into two Canadas, the population of Upper Canada exceeded 10,000.

John Graves Simcoe, Upper Canada's first Lieutenant-Governor, firmly believed that rapid settlement would persuade the territories west of the Alleghenies to return to the British fold. He liked to express the opinion that Upper Canada could become such a model of good government and economic opportunity that the original thirteen colonies would want to return to live under the British flag. But to achieve this, Simcoe maintained that a properly organized class structure supported by state and church institutions was necessary.

In 1792 Simcoe issued a proclamation through the British consul in Philadelphia advertising the availability of land in Upper Canada in the hope that Quakers would take advantage of the offer and come to the province as a group. Mennonites from Somerset County heard of the invitation and decided to act on it. A cohesive social and religious group, these Mennonites were the decendants of farmers who had already been highly successful as pioneers. They were willingly accepted and welcomed and arrived in 1794 to settle in Vaughan Township on the west side of Simcoe's Yonge Street, an area that had only been purchased from the Mississauga Indians a short six years before. Soon after, they were joined by a number of Dunkard settlers from the same Pennsylvania county.

By 1800 Mennonites from Franklin County had established a second settlement in an area known as the Beasley tract. This 60,000-acre parcel of land had been purchased jointly by a number of Mennonites who had formed the German Land Company for the express purpose of acquiring property in Upper Canada. Soon settlers from Lancaster and Montgomery counties joined those already there. This Waterloo settlement, far removed from existing centres, was destined to become the largest of the Mennonite communities in Ontario, and it maintained a greater degree of ethnic and religious isolation than the communities at Niagara or York County. Outside influences made few inroads on the culture that the Waterloo Mennonites had brought with them to Upper Canada.

Only a few years passed, however, before the legality of the Mennonites' title to the land at Waterloo came into question. It appeared that the land the Mennonites believed they had purchased in good faith from Richard Beasley still belonged to the Six Nations Confederacy of the Iroquois. Families en route to the tract when this dispute arose were redirected to Markham Township on the east side of Yonge Street in York County.

Some land in Markham Township had already been purchased by Mennonites from Lancaster County, Pennsylvania. Peter Reesor, for example, had been sent ahead by his father, Christian, to look for suitable property and had traded his horse and saddle for the land. Between the time of Peter's scouting expedition and the actual settlement of the Reesors in 1804, Mennonites from Montgomery County, originally destined for the Beasley tract, had made their way to the north part of the township. Henry Wideman and his family arrived as early as 1802, and the Mennonite meeting house in this settlement, the earliest in York County, was named after the Widemans.

In spite of harsh weather and dense forest the Mennonites in Upper Canada quickly began to clear land, plant crops, shelter the livestock, build homes and furniture and erect their meeting houses. Old customs and traditions allowed some semblance of a familiar way of life.[5] Barn-raisings and quilting bees provided an opportunity for isolated families to socialize, and births, weddings and deaths gave a familiar cadence to pioneer life, as did the unique customs which marked these events. Mennonites continued to practice the funeral custom of wrapping the dead in handmade shrouds, and weddings were sanctified in the homes rather than in the meeting places.

But tradition and custom could not protect the settlers from some of the discriminatory laws of their new country. One Canadian regulation required payment of a special tax, higher during time of war than in peace time, for military exemption. Another law disqualified Mennonites, Dunkards and Tunkers from certain duties because of their refusal to swear oaths. They were not, for example, allowed to serve as jurors or to give evidence in criminal court cases. Marriages had to be solemnized by a clergyman who had sworn an oath of allegiance, and since no Mennonite minister would do so, the Reverend William Jenkins, an

Anglican minister in the nearby town of Richmond Hill, performed marriage ceremonies for the Anabaptist settlers. Marriage vows were then repeated before one of the sect's own ministers.

York County was settled slowly. In 1825 there were still only thirty Mennonite families in Markham Township, but hard times in Pennsylvania soon sent many more across the border to swell the population of all three Mennonite settlements. Conservative Amish and Old Order Mennonites who went into the Waterloo area gave the Mennonites there their popular image — that of simple folk who wore austere clothing and who had little to do with the world outside their own community.

At the same time a number of Brethren in Christ families came to York County from Lancaster, Franklin and Lebanon counties in Pennsylvania. This sect, which grew up as a direct result of Mennonite influence, originated near the Susquehanna River, and in Pennsylvania adherents were called "River Brethren." In Upper Canada their baptism immersions earned them the name of Tunkers (the word in German means dipper). Although the sect had much in common with the Mennonites, it had a strong evangelical component, and members mingled freely with the British settlers in York County, paving the way for contact between the two major cultures in the county.

Various factors played a part in changing, if subtly and slowly, the distinct character of Mennonite life, especially in York County. In 1791, when Quebec had been divided into Upper and Lower Canada by the Constitutional Act, provision had been made for reserves of land to be set aside for both the Crown and the Church of England. These lands, which amounted to one-seventh part of each township for the clergy and one-seventh part to be held for the Crown as a means of raising funds to develop the colony, were scattered among the lots of the settlers. So instead of grouping together as they had done in Europe and later in America, the Mennonites were virtually isolated from one another. Acres of unused land held by speculators and the necessity of buying small individual parcels of land rather than large communal tracts further increased the isolation.

Farmsteads in York County were too far apart for the settler to depend on his neighbour for furniture-making or any other specialized skills, and he was forced to build his own furniture. Some had learned furniture-making skills in Pennsylvania, and the pieces made by these craftsmen show the fine American construction methods and designs. But the rude construction of some of the surviving pieces suggests that many Mennonite farmers were not particularly skilled in this area of endeavour. A great deal of the furniture they made was probably not considered worthy of a permanent place in the home, and when it could finally be replaced with more skilled construction, was either discarded or burned. The same is true of the early homes, many of which were either torn down to make way for more substantial dwellings or pressed into service as an outbuilding on the farm.

Isolation, a definite obstacle to specialization, meant that many skills were lost. But inevitably centuries-old designs and techniques were replaced by new ones as both Mennonite and non-Mennonite crafts-men slowly developed a furniture tradition of their own.

Because the York County Mennonite community was a small one, contact between Mennonites and non-Mennonites was inevitable, and this interaction was to have a profound effect on furniture-making in the community. "No article of manufacture could be purchased nearer than Little York; so that every man had to be his own mechanick, or exchange work with some of his ingenious neighbours."[6] Often these ingenious neighbours were non-Mennonites. William Beebe, an Eng-lishman, for instance, made tools for all of the householders in the south Markham area, and Mennonite housewives came to depend on the itinerant peddlars for housewares.

The saw, grist or hemp mill was another meeting place for the two cultures. These mills were only profitable if they served all of the settlers in the immediate environs. In Waterloo the Mennonite commu-nity was large enough to have its own mills, but in York the mills were shared. Mennonites and non-Mennonites also shared the churches which often doubled as schools during the week.

The city to the south was growing rapidly, and it affected the York County Mennonites in much the same way as Philadelphia had asserted its influence on the Mennonites in rural Pennsylvania. By 1850 Toronto boasted more than eighty cabinet-makers, mostly from England and Ireland, and twenty hardware dealers, who supplied machine-made British-styled hardware. Brown's Directory for 1856 lists eight pages of carpenters and a dozen furniture dealers in Toronto.

York County Mennonites were close enough to Toronto to be influenced by the city's modern (and often imported) ideas, yet far enough away to be able to retain some of their traditions and their religious identity. Unlike the relatively isolated Waterloo community, where furniture continued to be made as it had been in Pennsylvania, or Niagara, where urban influences overwhelmed the Pennsylvania tradition, York County furniture came to be a unique mixture of the traditional rural and the modern urban styles and construction methods.

(Left) Pennsylvania-style construction is evident in this early Markham Mennonite cupboard. It has the simple bracket feet, fielded panelled doors, abbreviated cornice and built-in look of the Pennsylvania pieces.

(Right) This handsome cherry and chestnut pegged cupboard is typical of the fine craftsmanship of the Bakers of Vaughan Township. As in most Dunkard furniture, there is no glass in the upper doors, and the framed base gives a built-in appearance. The piece was made by the younger Jonathan Baker ca. 1890.

Furniture made by John and Jacob Barkey mirrored the process of assimilation that was taking place in Markham Township by the mid-nineteenth century. This pine china cupboard, an example of John Barkey's early work, shows none of the Empire influences that were to distinguish the brothers' later work. The piece has never been painted.

(Left) This pine corner cupboard, made by a member of the Smith family of Vaughan Township, was paint-grained tan over cream. Originally, muslin curtains hung in the upper section.

(Right) This unusual pine cupboard was made in Markham and later taken to Waterloo. The double bank of three drawers and square panels in the lower doors give it a different appearance than most Markham cupboards. Note the quarter columns and ogee bracket feet. The piece is paint-grained brown over cream.

(Left) The rounded arches, Germanic bracket feet and apron and the three drawers make this corner cupboard a typical example of Waterloo construction. Made of pine and basswood, it was once painted red and green. The original knobs were replaced by handles which were in turn replaced by knobs similar to the original ones.

(Right) Walnut linen presses were among the finest pieces made by Niagara area craftsmen. This one, made ca. 1810, has lip-moulded drawers, the original, purchased hardware, square bracket feet and reeding on cornice and pilaster that distinguish it from the rustic traditions of Waterloo and York County. Possibly it was made in a furniture shop or factory, with different craftsmen working on the piece. It is of pegged construction, and knotholes in the wood on the sides have been expertly patched with matching pieces of walnut.

(Left) The elder Jonathan Baker built this large pine corner cupboard in 1853, seven years before his death. It is of pegged and forged-nail construction and has handmade walnut knobs. Both of the two small drawers can be locked.

(Right) The paint-graining on this pine cupboard, made in Waterloo ca. 1880, is far more stylized than that found on York County pieces. The wooden knobs, carved Germanic arches on the upper section, Germanic bracket feet and flattened cornice all distinguish it from cupboards made by the Barkey brothers in York County. The cupboard is brown over yellow.

(Left) Corner cupboards, especially those framed to appear built-in, are rare in Markham. This pine piece still has its original glass and hardware, including the exceptionally fine brass pulls on the top section. The drawer fronts are of bird's-eye maple, and the paint-grained decoration on the rest of the cupboard may once have matched the drawers.

(Right) This pegged pine corner cupboard from Waterloo has folk tulips carved in low relief on either side of the drawers. The piece originally was painted a solid colour and the tulips highlighted in contrasting colours. With its rounded arches and bracket feet the cupboard is very American in appearance. Note the unusual cornice.

(Left) This is almost certainly a later Barkey cupboard showing the full flowering of the Empire influence in the ogee-curved drawers and the beading trim around the drawers and cornice. The cupboard is pine and appears never to have been painted. It has the pie shelf and fluted feet common to Barkey pieces, but is narrower and more elegant than their early cupboards.

(Right) This pine china cupboard was made by one of the Barkey brothers, probably Jacob, ca. 1865. The pointed arches indicate a departure from the Pennsylvania tradition. In the nineteenth century a large drawer was created by combining two smaller drawers to provide enough space for storing linen tablecloths.

3 The Furniture and Its Makers

The Niagara Area

The early years of settlement in the Niagara area were difficult and precluded any unnecessary activity, but the craft of furniture-making seems to have come through this period relatively unscathed. In spite of the disruption caused by the move to the north, skills and techniques were retained and even improved, and only a slight lag in style resulted. In fact, many historians contend that permanent furniture of a high caliber was being made in this settlement within less than a decade of its purchase from the Indians. While this may be something of an overstatement, it does indicate how quickly the craft of furniture-making was re-established.

There were several reasons for this. Perhaps the most important was the continued contact with the American colonies. Not only were precision tools and sophisticated hardware available, but the latest styles in furniture came to the area even faster than they had once filtered into rural areas around Philadelphia. In addition, cabinet-makers from Europe and the eastern United States settled in the Niagara area, keeping the standards of furniture-making high. There was wealth in the area, too, and settlers who could afford to purchase goods provided a market for the products of early furniture factories. All of this activity exerted an enormous influence on the Mennonite craftsmen from Pennsylvania. Soon they too were making fine pieces that boasted metal mountings and were made from such woods as curly and bird's-eye maple, walnut and cherry — woods that country craftsmen had never before attempted to use so ambitiously.

The use of hard woods and the awareness of the latest neo-classical styles brought changes to the construction and design of the furniture. Carved decoration, such as narrow reeding on cornices and quarter columns, began to replace paint-graining and folk art decoration. The hard woods gave clarity and definition to styles that in thick pine would merely have appeared bulky. And as the craftsmen gained confidence and became more skilled in working with these woods, proportions changed somewhat, losing some of the Germanic heaviness and gaining a certain slim elegance.

Although it is doubtful that much of the built-in furniture favoured in America was constructed at Niagara, the Pennsylvania antecedents were obvious. The movable pieces, linen presses, tables with outside stretchers, blanket boxes with painted finishes, clock cases with broken arched Chippendale pediments, dish cupboards and chests of drawers, all remained faithful to their Pennsylvania models.

Niagara furniture continued to reflect the Chippendale style common in early Pennsylvania after it had declined in popularity in America. In its place American craftsmen had adopted the new classicism of the Regency style from England and, particularly, the Empire style from France. Mennonite furniture-makers in Niagara gradually began to absorb the new European classicism as it was interpreted by their counterparts in America, and within a quarter of a century the recognizably Germanic country tradition had been supplanted by Americanized Empire neo-classicism.

The Waterloo Area

In contrast to the uninterrupted furniture-making tradition of Niagara, furniture-making in Waterloo was suspended during the early years of the nineteenth century as pioneers poured their energies into clearing land, building shelter for livestock and putting farms on a firm operational basis. The first furniture in this isolated pioneer settlement was hastily made with crude tools, strictly functional rather than decorative and probably discarded as soon as it could be replaced with something sturdier and more attractive. But the Waterloo settlement grew quickly, and within a single generation skills that had grown rusty with disuse and almost-forgotten methods of construction were put back into practice, and permanent furniture was again produced.

Whereas in Niagara furniture grew out of an American tradition and continued to develop along parallel lines, gradually incorporating the neo-classicism popular in America, in Waterloo furniture-making remained more firmly rooted in the Pennsylvania past. When classical styles finally found their way to Waterloo, some of the features appeared along side those of older styles, sometimes within a single piece of furniture. This blend of styles produced a furniture that can only be called "country classical."

The constant influx of settlers from Pennsylvania (halted only during the brief time of the title dispute and during the War of 1812) meant that the colonial basis of the Waterloo tradition grew stronger over the years and that new developments in Pennsylvania were brought to Waterloo soon after they were in use there. This continuous emigration also swelled the already sizeable Mennonite settlement so that craftsmen who decided to specialize in furniture-making were assured of a market for their products.

Settlers also moved to Waterloo from Niagara, bringing the Americanized Empire style and new techniques, such as stencilling, with them. And the old techniques of veneering and inlay work were refreshed through this constant, if indirect, contact with Pennsylvania.

Paint was used, as it had been in Pennsylvania, to add decoration to plain pieces, but in Waterloo it also frequently disguised rough workmanship, at least in the early years. Painted or inlaid folk symbols were common, but there was little attempt to duplicate the grains of more desirable woods, a technique common in America. Paint-graining was usually done in a fanciful, stylized fashion using bright colours that often bore little resemblance to the woods they were duplicating. Occasionally folk symbols were carved in low relief and highlighted in paint of contrasting colours, with the rest of the piece painted a solid colour.

Waterloo furniture remained more Germanic than that of the other Upper Canada Mennonite settlements. The bracket feet on Waterloo pieces were uniquely Germanic, as were the bun feet which, although smaller than those used on the Pennsylvania *kas* and *schranke*, appeared frequently on Waterloo pieces. The shaping or scalloping of cornices and aprons and the rounded arches found on many cupboard doors were also typical of rural Pennsylvania pieces and had their roots in Europe.

Almost all of the furniture in Waterloo was made of soft pine as it had been in Pennsylvania. Occasionally, panels in cupboards or cabinets or the drawer fronts on chests of drawers were made of butternut or basswood, but hard woods such as walnut are only occasionally seen in the furniture which survives today.

In general, Waterloo furniture, unlike that of Niagara, had few pretensions to grandness. Its proportions were as rectangular and earthy as they had been in Europe and America, and the furniture fulfilled the same simple functions. Even when the furniture tradition in Waterloo matured, there was little attempt to reproduce the fine styles of the Niagara craftsmen. After Waterloo furniture-makers recaptured the skills that had lain dormant for a generation, they continued to make pieces that were delightfully picturesque rather than elegant, using folk art decoration to give the pieces charm and beauty.

Unfortunately a great deal of the furniture made in the Waterloo community has been removed and sold in the United States as Pennsylvania furniture. The close resemblance between the two made it a prime target for antique dealers looking for pieces to satisfy the American desire for artifacts from their colonial past. It was not until 1967, when Canadians celebrated their centennial and began to take an interest in the furniture of the early years, that this practice finally subsided. It can only be assumed that the pieces most similar to those of Pennsylvania were the first to be hurried out of the province and that the American influence on Waterloo furniture was even stronger than the pieces found today in Canadian museums and homes indicate.

York County

York County was the smallest of the Mennonite communities in Upper Canada and, at least in Markham where the major portion of the York Mennonites settled, was the last to resume a furniture-making tradition. Half a century and more than one generation were to lapse before York craftsmen began to make furniture intended to be permanent or before specialization of furniture-making skills was considered a reasonably viable and profitable undertaking. But by the 1840s prosperity in the farming areas of the province provided the impetus that was needed. Large new homes were built, and the demand arose for attractive as well as functional furniture.

If there were reasons for the Markham Mennonites' slowness in resuming furniture-building, they appear not to have had an adverse effect on the other furniture-makers in the county. Craftsmen outside the Mennonite community brought skills with them and used them continuously. William Keffer (1812-1897), for instance, was a German Lutheran whose family had come to Vaughan Township from Pennsylvania in 1806. Keffer made finely-crafted furniture, working in woods other than pine and even veneering some pieces extensively. One table made by Keffer has a veneered pedestal base and is thoroughly Regency in style. Quite probably Keffer modelled it on the furniture of British settlers who had come to the county.

Soon after the Quakers arrived in the north part of the county they too began to make handsome furniture.[1] A York County dissident off-shoot of the Quakers, the Children of Peace, attracted craftsmen to their group who were widely talented in a variety of disciplines including music and painting. The furniture made by some members was of such attractive woods as curly maple and incorporated surprisingly up-to-date facets of European design. The work of John Doan, a cabinet-maker, is still on display in the Children of Peace Sharon Temple. It is as fine as any furniture found anywhere in Ontario.

Some of the Dunkards or German Baptists who came to Vaughan Township from Pennsylvania also brought furniture-making skills with them to the new land. These skills were passed on from generation to generation with scarcely any interruption. Unlike the Markham Mennonites, the Dunkards intermarried with Tunkers, Mennonites and non-Anabaptists in Vaughan, sharing skills and methods and thus keeping them alive.

The Pennsylvania tradition dominated Dunkard furniture, making it even more rural American in style than Waterloo furniture. Like the Pennsylvania pieces, Dunkard furniture had turned, wooden, mushroom-shaped pulls or small wooden buttons. Drawers in most china cupboards came in sets of three, a characteristic of German furniture that had been transplanted to Pennsylvania. Built-in furniture and movable cupboards often had framed bases that went to the floor to make them look built-in. Dunkard craftsmen occasionally worked in woods other than pine, which suggests that they were confident of their abilities, but seldom used paint decoration or carved ornamentation.

One of the most accomplished of the Vaughan Dunkard craftsmen was Jonathan Baker, who had come from Somerset County, Pennsylvania, in 1816 at the age of twenty-four. A years-long journey, during which Baker's grandfather who was travelling in a separate wagon was lost, finally ended with the arrival of the rest of the family at a 200-acre piece of land purchased for £225. Jonathan Baker began to make furniture for all of the members of his family soon after he arrived in the county. His furniture had the wooden pulls, framed bases and panelled doors that were typical of Dunkard furniture in Pennsylvania. Although most pieces had little in the way of decoration except fine proportions and smooth fielded panels, the single instance of inlay found in the country has been attributed to him. On one of the small chests of drawers he made, inlaid stars surround each of the brown flint knobs.

Baker built in a great deal of his furniture, even cutting down pediments on dry sinks to make them fit around kitchen windows and sometimes leaving unfinished the ends of pieces that were to go against the wall. A versatile craftsman, he also made the locks and hardware that were used on his furniture. Jonathan Baker died childless in 1860, but his nephew Jesse and Jesse's son, Jonathan, were the recipients of his furniture-making skills.

The Bakers' furniture, although plain, has an authority and simplicity that is very pleasing to the eye. All three made large corner cupboards, small corner and hanging cabinets and built-in sets of drawers as the Dunkards had done in Pennsylvania. Instead of carving or painted symbols, simple fielded panels decorated their pieces. By the time the younger Jonathan Baker was making the furniture for the family (and he did for many years, finishing one cupboard the day he turned eighty), he was skilled enough to work in more difficult woods than the usual pine and was using peg and screw construction. His skill in design and construction can be seen in the cupboards he made for his seven children, each in different styles and types of wood.

The Cobers, who at various times through the generations were members of the Dunkard and Brethren in Christ sects, were related to the Bakers through marriage and shared their furniture-making skills. Peter Cober, the bishop of the Cober Church in Vaughan, made spinning wheels (as did the first Jonathan Baker) for his family and members of his congregation. He, and possibly his father Nicholas, also made chairs in the Pennsylvanian style, with intricately turned front legs, slat backs and wedged front posts going right through the arm.

Like the Bakers, the Cobers passed their skills on to succeeding generations. Toward the end of the nineteenth century Benjamin Cober, although primarily a farmer, was making furniture to order for members of the Brethren in Christ congregation at Heise Hill in Markham. A cupboard made by Cober suggests that some of the Germanic traits of Pennsylvania furniture had been lost after the time of Jonathan Baker and Peter Cober. It has two drawers instead of the usual Germanic three and is altogether smaller and lighter in appearance than Pennsylvania cupboards. It has a peg closing, nailed rather than dove-tailed drawers and a delicately carved apron and cornice. A dry sink also made by Ben Cober is smaller than those made by previous furniture-makers in the county and has an Empire-style pediment. The dry sink and cupboard were made by Cober for English settlers who had become members of the Brethren in Christ sect after coming to the county, and the pieces may have been commissioned to be built in the style these English settlers favoured.

Two other Dunkard furniture-makers of note were Henry Snider and his son Jacob who made furniture in styles similar to those of rural Pennsylvania from pine trees on the family's property in both Vaughan and York townships.[2] The Sniders were German Baptists from Lancaster County and had moved to Upper Canada a year before Henry was born in 1807. Henry Snider's grandfather, according to a study done on the family, had been "a skillful mechanic, a blacksmith, a silversmith, a gunsmith and at times a bellsmith."[3] His father Samuel had learned blacksmithing while still in his teens and had made furniture decorated with the paint-graining and geometric symbols common in Pennsylvania. Henry in turn passed all of these skills on to his son Jacob, teaching him blacksmithing and carpentry in the workshop on the property in Vaughan.

The pieces made by father and son have pedestal bases or simple bracket feet, fielded panelled doors and handmade knobs common to Pennsylvania German furniture. One of his chests of drawers shows the only example of bun feet on a large piece found in York County. But some of the Sniders' designs indicate a departure from the old ways. A cupboard made by the senior Snider has two instead of the usual three drawers and glass panes in the upper doors. He often worked in bird's-eye maple or cherry rather than pine and frequently added turned split balusters or carved pediments to case pieces.

Jacob's furniture was as carefully constructed as that of his father and often showed a good deal of ingenuity and character: one of his tables has a top which turns and opens to become a double-sized surface; another has a hinged top that lifts to reveal space for writing materials so that the piece can also be used as a desk; a step stool cleverly unfolds into a chair; a pine secretary is fitted in the middle section with numerous pigeon-holes behind a drop surface and has an additional section with glass doors above this.

The Sniders intermarried with the Smiths, one of the earliest Mennonite families in Vaughan. While Jacob Smith also made furniture for his family in the early years of the settlement, he seems not to have had the background of family expertise the Sniders, Bakers and Cobers had. In spite of this, the ingenuity of Smith's carpentry is evident, particularly in one piece from the original Smith home. It is a wet sink, with a drain that leads to the floor from the basin section of the sink. This drain was once attached to pipes that ran through the wall of the log home to carry water away.

Much of the record of the settlement in Vaughan disappeared when the land where the earliest Mennonite settlers lived was purchased by the CNR and the homes were torn down. The evidence that does remain suggests that early Mennonite furniture was made by relatively unskilled craftsmen, who paid less attention to detail than to speed. The few pieces remaining in Vaughan township have typically Germanic proportions and little in the way of decoration except for a paint-grained finish. Furniture made by later generations of Vaughan Mennonites was, like Dunkard furniture, very similar to that made in rural Pennsylvania.

The Mennonites in Markham Township at first maintained a certain aloofness from surrounding pockets of settlement. They seem to have had little contact, for instance, with the Quakers who had come from the same Pennsylvania counties and settled just a township north of them. Although conditions forced association with settlers of other cultures, the Markham Mennonites steadfastly resisted assimilation. There were strict prohibitions against intermarriage, for instance, and anyone defying the custom was excommunicated by the church and ostracized by the community. Although not as conservative as some of the Waterloo Mennonites, they had strong feelings about preserving their way of life. Years later their attitudes toward automobiles illustrated the differences between the two groups. Some of the conservative Waterloo Mennonites did without cars (and still do), while the Markham Mennonites bought and used them. But for many years the latter bought only black cars and then painted all of the chrome black.

Little permanent furniture was made in the early years in Markham, and over this period of time much of the Pennsylvania tradition was lost. For a while most furniture in Markham was strictly functional with no decorative touches to it. Flour bins, dry sinks and cupboards were put together in the simplest possible way, as were cradles which might have a single heart carved into the headboard for decoration. Tables were made in the simple styles that had been popular in Pennsylvania with a single board top and turned legs. Usually the householder made his own furniture, and he had neither the time nor, in many cases, the specialized skills to add decorative features. In its simplicity the furniture of early Markham bears a good deal of resemblance to the earliest furniture of Pennsylvania.

But there were some exceptions. Clock cases, for example, were finely crafted and likely intended to be permanent. Usually clockworks were brought from Pennsylvania by wagon, while the bulky cases were left behind. Soon after the settlers arrived at their destination, new cases were made in American styles, with the broken arched pediments and bracket feet common in Pennsylvania cases. The craftsmanship of pieces still in the area was less sure than that of the American pieces, but the builders' lack of precision tools may account for this.

In the years following the initial settlement, when old traditions had been lost and not yet replaced by new ones, some of the furniture in Markham was assembled rather than crafted. Chairs, for example, were sometimes made by Mennonite tradesmen who bought bundles of turned members from larger companies such as Jacques and Hays.[4] The chair-maker might buy all of the parts and put the chairs together, or he might fit the purchased turned members to slab seats he had made himself.

Abram Ramer, the earliest full-time furniture-maker known in Markham, may have begun his career by assembling chairs. One chair very likely made by him has the date 1833 carved into the underside of the seat. It is a straightforward arrow-back with a pine slab seat and elm legs. Ramer eventually built a factory where he made chairs and window sashes. By 1856 he had made a great deal of progress and advertised himself in the Markham *Economist and Sun* that year as the operator of a "furniture wareroom" as well as a cabinet-maker and upholsterer.[5] To date, no large pieces made by Ramer have been found, nor is it known whether other members of the family also worked in the factory.

Abram Ramer's rise from sash- and chair-maker to cabinet-maker paralleled the course that the craft of furniture-making took in the township as a whole. Prosperity in the middle of the century gave rise to a building boom which produced many fine, large homes and some of the most exciting furniture ever made in the county. By this time, however, some of the niceties of Pennsylvania design and decoration had been forgotten and something new had to be found to fill the gap. The authoritative and impressive Empire style being adopted by other settlers in the area and by Mennonites in the other settlements in the province seemed a suitable and logical place to start.

When Mennonite craftsmen in Markham finally began to build furniture for people outside their immediate families, it was different from anything ever made before by rural craftsmen. The pronounced and showy features of the Empire style were added to the massive Germanic rectangular cases with a maximum of drama and gusto.

Several factors abetted this transition in furniture, making the plain and homely more dramatic. For one thing, the Mennonites in Markham were beginning to have more contact with other settlers in the community. Some had given up the German language and some had even drifted away from the church. Their reluctance to involve themselves in civic affairs was at an end, and they became respected and prominent members of an established community. One such citizen, David Reesor, illustrates the dramatic changes the community as a whole was undergoing. A descendant of the original Reesor pioneers, he had joined the United Church, was made a senator and established the Markham newspaper, the *Economist and Sun*.

Secondly, there was much less emigration into Markham from Pennsylvania than there was at Waterloo, and the styles of the original settlement were gradually forgotten. Another small but important factor in the transition was the fact that precision tools, supplied by non-Mennonites in the area, were available to the community. Finally, the large new homes that were being built for Mennonites, sometimes by non-Mennonite masons or bricklayers, were so impressive that they seemed to need equally impressive furniture.

The large pieces, such as the china cupboards and chests of drawers given to children as wedding gifts, formed the basis of the new furniture tradition. These were the most imposing pieces and the ones most ostentatiously paint-grained to resemble the woods used by the makers of Empire furniture.

The craftsmen who were most responsible for these new directions were two brothers, John and Jacob Barkey, who probably began to specialize in making furniture for Mennonites other than their own families just before the middle of the nineteenth century. Mennonite parents contracted them to make gifts for their children who were about to be married. The Barkeys made the same item for each child in a family, whether a china cupboard or chest of drawers and matching blanket box. Since these wedding gifts were special, the most elaborate decorative flourishes were added to them.

With its sweeping Empire flourishes on pine country pieces, Barkey furniture was a unique departure from what had gone before. Even the Pennsylvania characteristics were incorporated with such flair that they seem entirely compatible with the Empire additions. The shell motif of American colonial furniture, for example, was used on Empire pediments of chests of drawers and became an integral part of this new hybrid style. Although it is not always possible to tell which of the brothers made a particular piece, it is impossible to see one of their works and not know that one of them made it.

Barkey cupboards are always flat-to-the-wall rather than corner cupboards. They are of forged nail construction, and the drawers are put together with series of small handmade dovetails. Their sides are not panelled, and the absence of cracking and warping illustrates the Barkey competence at basic construction. Each of the cupboards has an identical pie shelf in the space between the upper and lower parts of the piece. Cornices are single-board cyma-curved in contrast to the double-board extended cornices of Waterloo cupboards. Lower doors have fielded panels with the modified pointed Gothic arch of British furniture, rather than the rounded arch of Germanic and Waterloo furniture. This pointed arch is repeated around the glass panes in the upper doors. Shelves inside the upper part of the unit seldom meet the framing of the glass panes of the doors in early Barkey cupboards, and a movable spoon rack contributes to this asymmetry. Front feet usually are finished in a tapered ogee bracket that reflected the Hepplewhite influence.

Except for a slight shaping of the apron, there is no carved decoration on the early Barkey cupboards, and neither painted folk art nor relief-carved symbols ever appear on any Barkey furniture. For all their competence, the Barkeys were too far removed from a strong furniture-making tradition that might have taught them how to work in the more difficult hard woods. So the cupboards, always made of pine, were usually paint-grained to imitate the harder woods associated with Empire furniture, with the graining colours exactly duplicating the wood colour. The woods they most often imitated were walnut, cherry, bird's-eye maple and mahogany.

In a cupboard that is almost certainly a later example of Barkey construction, even more of the Germanic-Pennsylvania traits have been discarded. The cupboard has only two drawers, a striking departure in itself, and both have an ogee curve to them in the Empire style. Beading trim around the cornice and drawers and a delicate shaping to the apron are the only other decoration. The cupboard still has the pointed arch to the doors, but the shelves now meet the line of the glass panes.

Chests of drawers made by the Barkeys are even more influenced by the Empire style. Pediments are in the chimney-pot style or flamboyantly scrolled and often have the shell motif carved at the centre. Split balusters attached to the pilasters further the Empire style, and these balusters are usually a repetition of the shape of the turned foot. Barkey furniture has idiosyncrasies as well as character; the panelled sides of chests of drawers, for instance, were sometimes dissimilarly grained. These massive (over five-and-a-half-feet) pieces have five drawers, with the top two small drawers often overhanging the other three in the Empire fashion. The lower drawers are in an ascending order of size, with the bottom drawer almost as large as the European blanket chests from which they derived. Drawer fronts were often painted in imitation bird's-eye maple.

Unlike true Empire furniture, Barkey pieces had neither metal ornamentation or mountings. Even if these had been commonly available, they probably would have made the pieces too expensive for the thrifty Mennonite farmers who paid only $7.50 for Barkey china cupboards. Instead, mountings were locally-purchased, brown flint enamel pottery or white ceramic with cast-iron pulls. From a distance the brown enamel pulls resembled a dark burled hard wood and may have been used on some pieces to give that effect. Both types of pulls were available locally between 1850 and 1870.

The Barkeys also made many blanket boxes, sometimes painting them to match a chest of drawers. Often, though, these straightforward boxes with their flat surfaces prompted the Barkeys to perform the most dashing feats of paint-graining. Many of them were painted in such a way that they appeared to be inlaid, with borders resembling one type of wood and inset panels another type or another section from a different part of the same tree.

Unlike similar pieces from the Waterloo area, Barkey blanket boxes had little or no decoration, except for this paint-graining. Painted folk art designs were never used and pieces were rarely even signed. The only carving was in the shaping of the apron. In construction, they were as simple as the Pennsylvania blanket boxes. The sides were fitted together with series of small handmade dovetails and with a small till at one end of the inside. Few had drawers beneath the section used to store blankets and quilts, although several of this type have been found in York County.

Simeon Reesor (1829-1909), a Markham craftsman, built furniture at about the same time as the Barkeys. Reesor was a builder of coffins and caskets, and his furniture shows a simplicity and economy of line that may be traceable to his primary occupation. Pieces made by him show few of the exuberant Empire flourishes of the Barkeys' work, but are just as remote from the Pennsylvania tradition. They have no folk art decoration of any kind and are stained rather than paint-grained to resemble harder woods. They do, however, show some of the slim, almost Sheratonesque lines that were often found in the simplest Pennsylvania furniture and later in many Waterloo pieces. Generally, Reesor furniture is smaller, simpler and more graceful than Barkey furniture.

A desk made by Simeon Reesor in 1890 shows the sure craftsmanship of this furniture-maker. It is perfectly plain except for its panelled doors and drop leaf and the slight shaping of the apron. Inside, its compartments are finished as beautifully as the exterior of the piece, with the pine stained to resemble walnut. A table made by Reesor circa 1850 has tapered, squared legs supporting a single pine top-board, twenty-three inches wide, and its drawers are highlighted by applewood knobs.

Reesor began to make furniture around the time of his marriage in 1851, and while he made numerous pieces for his own household, it is uncertain whether he ever made furniture for other members of the community. However Reesor furniture has been found in a number of Markham homes, suggesting that he might have taken up furniture-building as a commercial venture.

The new tradition begun by the Barkeys was carried further a generation later by Samuel Burkholder, a nephew of the Barkey brothers. The Burkholders, who had come to the township in 1833, three years before Samuel's birth, operated a store in the Stouffville area of Markham where they both made and sold furniture. Like the Ramers, the Burkholders may have begun by assembling pieces of turned furniture that were shipped to them from larger factories. In any case, by the time Samuel Burkholder began to make furniture, he had an established market and was thus able to make a wider range of pieces than had the Barkeys. In fact, while the Barkeys had only made the larger pieces that were given as gifts, Burkholder was able to make all of the pieces that were used in the home, and for the first time, these pieces of lesser importance became fully a part of the Mennonite furniture tradition in Markham.

But where the Barkeys had added their own interpretation of Empire elegance to their furniture, Burkholder was truer to the exact letter of the British style. Although he worked in the softer woods, primarily pine, he stained his furniture to look like walnut. And he used the cast-iron pulls that were then available in the country to give even minor kitchen pieces a finer look.

Furniture-making tools were more accessible by this time, and the carving found on Burkholder's large pieces was done by machine in his factory-cum-store. This standardization of technique eliminated the individuality which had been a trademark of the Barkey pieces and gave his furniture a somewhat mass-produced look. Burkholder furniture was also smaller and lighter looking than furniture made by the Barkeys.

There is no evidence to suggest that Burkholder used paint-graining to decorate his furniture, but towards the end of his career he did begin to add Victorian decorative features. This brought a new sobriety and decorum to his pieces, further removing them from the rustic Pennsylvania tradition.

Burkholder was the last furniture-maker of importance in the township. His furniture both moulded opinion and reflected the new taste for machine-made styles. Markham Mennonites wanted the real thing, and when they could afford it, they began to buy factory-made British furniture from Toronto stores as well as local machine-made furniture. Spool beds became highly prized items and were often purchased as part of a set to match chests of drawers with turned spool pilasters. Gradually machine-made cupboards and tables replaced those which had been hand made in the area, and horsehair upholstered furniture took the place of wooden chairs and benches.

But the handmade pieces were kept and cherished both for their sentimental value and for their historic worth. Frequently pieces from Niagara or Waterloo found their way into York County homes, brought by brides when they married, and these, too, were saved. When the railway went through in 1872, brides also came from the United States, occasionally bringing pieces from home with them.

One Pennsylvania-made chest of drawers shipped to Markham by rail shows characteristics that were never recovered by Markham craftsmen. It was made by Abraham Krider in 1885 for Rebecca Miller, who came to Markham to marry a descendant of the Reesors. The pine case is completely veneered in cherry and has pressed glass knobs. The upper drawer front is veneered with cross-cut cherry, cut from where the branch meets the trunk of the tree, and the lower three drawers are veneered in butt-cut cherry, cut from the stump of the tree. Decoration on the piece consists of handmade beading trim around the top drawer and deeply-carved pilasters. It is much smaller than the chests of drawers that were made by the Barkeys at the same time, and shows how Empire features were gradually absorbed into a long-established furniture tradition, in contrast to Barkey furniture, which took the Empire styling and made it the basis for something new.

Although the Mennonites often brought clockworks with them from their American settlements, they rarely brought the clock cases. However one case found in Markham was made in Maryland about the middle of the eighteenth century. A hundred years later it was shipped to Markham by rail, and when it arrived it was found to have been transported full of books. The case is unique in that it has a hole in the side where a string can be pulled to make the clock strike the last hour. These pieces of furniture from other Mennonite communities were not only tangible reminders of home, but were considered finer than local pieces and because of this were given pride of place in the new home.

Fortunately, a Mennonite custom has helped to keep the old furniture in the community. When the head of a Mennonite household dies, his or her furnishings are usually portioned out to the surviving members of the family according to the provisions of a will. If no will has been made or if certain pieces are not mentioned specifically, a family sale is held, and the immediate family bids on the pieces they want to keep. If a family sale is unfeasible, a public sale is held, and Mennonites from all over the area attend in the hopes of buying the furniture and keeping it in the community. New owners acquire not only the piece of furniture but also any information about it that is known, such as who made it, who its owners have been, what homes it has stood in and how old it is. Although this custom did not succeed in keeping furniture in Waterloo (many dealers were anxious to acquire the pieces and many Mennonites were eager to sell pieces whose historic value they were not aware of), a general lack of interest in York County Mennonite furniture meant that it was often bought by Mennonites of the community.

Church furniture in York County is radically different from other furniture in the settlement. Whereas household furniture gladly embraced the sophistication and exuberance of new styles and new ideas, meeting house furniture was made a century earlier in the plainest, most austere style possible. Benches with decorative shaping have been found in one church in the area, but these are the exceptions. Decoration was seldom used and most pieces were not even painted or varnished. Through their church furniture, the Mennonites expressed the simple, basic Christian tenets in which they believed.

Most churches had a minimum of basic pieces. Usually in the front of the church there was a plain, one-drawer table with a Bible stand which served as a pulpit and a straight-back wooden chair. The pine benches for the congregation had a single board across the back and a single plank for the seat, and a long bench separated the men's from the women's side of the church. The choir, which provided the only music heard in Mennonite churches, sat on plain benches facing the ministerial table at right angles to the rest of the congregation. In a separate room or gallery on the women's side of the church, double cradles were used to rock two infants to sleep at the same time. Meeting house furniture was made communally by members of the congregation, and since accounts were seldom kept, little is known of the cost or the makers.

When the churches were first built, they were used only in daylight hours and no provision was made for lighting or heating. Later, wall brackets or ceiling fixtures for oil lamps and wood-burning stoves were added to make the buildings more comfortable.

The churches had no ornamentation of any kind beyond these simple furnishings, but the absence of pictures, brightly-painted walls and stained glass made for an austerity that gave the setting a simple beauty.

From the beginning York County Anabaptists were conservationists and recyclers of both church and household furniture. When the churches were raised to give them basements, the original benches were used downstairs for Sunday schools, and new ones were made for the main part of the church.

Similarly, home furniture was changed to accommodate progress. In one Vaughan home a corner cupboard of round-peg and forged-nail construction made by Jonathan Baker was equipped with an electric outlet rather than moved when the house was electrified. It is not uncommon to find china cupboards like the ones made by the Barkey brothers repainted at intervals over the years and regrained to resemble the original finish. In one Barkey china cupboard two of the three original drawers were combined to make one large and one small drawer. The purpose of this was to provide a wide enough drawer to accommodate the large linen tablecloths favoured by the owner of the piece.

Fortunately the people of Vaughan and Markham are the most avid of amateur historians. Most of the old families have one member in each generation who spends spare hours chronicling the family's past and present. This sense of history is one of the major factors in preserving the furniture of York County (which is recognized as one particular kind of chronicle) and in hoarding the available information about pieces that were seldom signed or dated. Although furniture is no longer made by hand in the community on a large scale, the present generation still values the old pieces as tangible evidence of an historic past.

This set of nineteen small drawers was constructed by the younger Jonathan Baker (1831-1916). The drawers are of pine with the drawer fronts of cherry. The wooden knobs, common in Pennsylvania, are flat to the drawers, and the lower six drawers have wooden closers. The entire unit is screwed into the wall.

Dunkard craftsmen built-in a great deal of their furniture, and even movable pieces were constructed in such a way that they had a built-in look, or so that they exactly fitted a particular place in the home. This kitchen cabinet made by Jonathan Baker has been cut so that it will fit around a window.

(Opposite) Hanging cupboards were popular with Dunkard furniture-makers in Vaughan Township as they had been in Pennsylvania. The top section of this corner cabinet is older than the bottom part of the unit. Note the framing around the top section and the details of the pegged construction. The piece is pine, but is stained a darker colour.

(Top) Although its maker is not known for certain, this pine blanket box with its bracket feet and shaped apron is typical of those made by the Barkey brothers. It is extravagantly paint-grained to simulate inlaid woods.

The furniture-making tradition in the Niagara area quickly became sophisticated, but examples of rustic pieces can still be found. This Vineland box, decorated with folk art in the Pennsylvania fashion, is green and yellow on black, and the owner's name, Elizabeth Smith, is painted on the lid. The box has a framed base and is smaller in size than those found in York County.

York County Mennonite furniture was rarely made from woods other than pine but this chest of drawers with four finished feet is one of the exceptions. The sides are of maple and the drawer fronts of bird's-eye maple with pine as the secondary wood. The warping of the top of the chest suggests that the Markham craftsman was inexperienced in working with hard woods.

Stained to resemble walnut rather than paint-grained, this pine desk is a fine example of the later work of Simeon Reesor. It was constructed in 1890 and shows the economy of line that was Reesor's hallmark.

Abraham Krider made this chest of drawers for Rebecca Miller in Pennsylvania in 1855. In 1885 it was shipped to Markham by rail. Cherry veneer covers the pine case, and the beading around the top drawer is handmade. The knobs are of pressed glass.

This colourful chest of drawers is one of the finest examples of John Barkey's work. The Empire styling is obvious in the shape of the foot, the split balusters, the scrolled pediment and the overhanging top small drawers. The chest of drawers is red over cream, and the design of the paint-graining on one side is entirely different than that on the other. The piece was made in 1862 or 1863 of mortise and tenon, square nail and wooden peg construction.

This chest of drawers was made ca. 1855, probably by Jacob Barkey. Like most Barkey chests, the drawers are in a descending order of size. The scrolled Empire-style pediment with the shell motif at the centre also indicates Barkey construction as does the extravagant paint-graining and the four finished, trumpet-shaped turned feet. The knobs are of brown flint pottery.

John Barkey made this pine, forged-nail chest of drawers for Elizabeth Barkey in 1859. The dramatically scrolled pediment shows the Barkey interpretation of the Empire style, and the feet and the split balusters attached to the pilasters are also in the Empire mode. The piece is entirely paint-grained, with the two small overhanging drawers grained to resemble bird's-eye and the bottom drawer given a grained border to simulate inlay.

These two beds, once in Mennonite homes, are now in the Markham Museum. The larger one (ca. 1840) has lathe-turned posts and mushroom-shaped pegs that support a rope lacing. The trundle bed (ca. 1820) was crudely made of butted construction. It has handmade wooden wheels for moving it from beneath a larger one.

Both Mennonites and Dunkards favoured these lathe-turned beds in the early years in York County. This one has pine head and foot boards and mushroom-shaped pegs on a frame which was laced with rope to support a straw tick or mattress. It is still in use in a Dunkard home in Vaughan township.

(*Opposite top*) Double cradles were common in churches and meeting houses in Upper Canada. Two infants could be rocked to sleep in this pine cradle that was once in the original Wideman meeting house. It is now in the Markham Museum.

(*Opposite*) When this turned settle with its solid back board was constructed ca. 1875 it was used near the fireplace or stove. Nowadays many Mennonite homes have these comfortable pieces on front porches. This one was in the Barkey family for many years and may have been made by one of the Barkey furniture-makers.

Wheat gave the farmers of southern Ontario prosperity but flax gave the Mennonite farm wife cloth for numerous household necessities. This spinning wheel was used to spin flax into linen.

The date 1852 is carved on the underside of this pine sewing stand. It was made by a Mennonite farmer for his four daughters, and their initials are carved on the sides of the base. It has a unique pegged construction joining the top part of the stand to the base.

Christian Reesor brought this domed horsechair chest with leather bindings and brass studs to Markham in 1804. It contained recipes of folk remedies for a variety of complaints, a necessity in the wilds of Upper Canada. Today it also contains the Crown Deed to the land.

(Left) Settlers in early Markham and Vaughan had to depend on itinerant peddlers or the merchants at "Little York" for household implements. This cast-iron sewing bird is one of the early manufactured items. By depressing the tail the beak opened to hold fabric.

4 The Homes and Meeting Houses

Just as European furniture traditions were brought from America to Upper Canada by the Mennonites and there reshaped and reinterpreted, so, too, were architectural styles affected by the move into the new land. And always, like the furniture, the homes and churches had things to say about the cultural and social milieu of these people and about their past.

In Pennsylvania the earliest dwellings were caves dug into hillsides, and the first houses were small cabins.[1] Log cabins were first built in Pennsylvania by Swedish settlers who were assimilated to such an extent that their building traditions were generally overwhelmed by the influx of Germans and English into the colony. The Swedish cabin had a fireplace in one corner of the structure, while the Germanic cabin which came later had a fireplace that divided the cabin into one large and one small room, with the chimney emerging near the centre of the roof. Log cabins made by English settlers had a fireplace at either end of the structure so that chimneys emerged at each gable end. While the English cabin was square, the Germanic cabin was rectangular, ranging in size from twelve to sixteen feet in depth and from sixteen to twenty-four feet in width across the front. The first Germanic cabins were built of round, bark-covered logs and were roofed in oak or ash shingle, bark or thatch. They consisted of a lower storey, usually floored in clay, and an upper sleeping loft under the eaves. Skins or pieces of linen covered the window openings.

Later log homes were built larger, often rising two and a half storeys.

They had the same rectangular shape and central chimney as the earlier Germanic cabins and were built of oak or pine logs, sometimes squared or dressed on one or two sides.

Stone cabins, which became popular next, had been common in the Palatinate and Alsace. These had thick walls and narrow windows, and the chimney emerged near the centre of the roof in the typical Germanic fashion. Sometimes they were constructed in a bank style, with one or more sides of the building built into a hillside. The availability of local stone prompted many settlers to build stone homes, many of them large.

Later stone homes, often built onto existing smaller ones, were plain dwellings in a decidedly Germanic style. They had a door to one side on the long front wall, asymmetrical window placement with windows sometimes arched and often a basement with an arched stone entrance-way and a floor of handmade tiles. (Tile-making was one of the crafts gradually forgotten or abandoned by Mennonites long before the move to Upper Canada.) These homes continued to have the steeply-pitched, occasionally tiled roofs common to the earlier stone houses, although the roof pitch was later reduced when the Georgian style began to influence construction. Pent roofs were built on column-supported porches or on the verandahs which sometimes encircled the first storey.

At first Georgian features, such as carved doorways and solid shutters, were added to the basic Germanic rectangle. Later some Georgian features were built into the structure. Doors and windows, for instance, began to be more symmetrically placed and more elaborately conceived. Chimneys were often placed at the gable ends of the houses in the English manner, and porches with classical columns were added. Sometimes the stone walls were covered with stucco or plaster, a common Germanic practice, in a variety of pastel shades.

Frame houses were also common in some counties in rural Pennsylvania. Inner and outer walls were enclosed with boards and filled with shale, sawdust or straw for insulation. Brick homes became popular when bricks began to be made in wooden, handmade molds from clay found on the property. In Pennsylvania it was common to paint brick houses, including painted lines to simulate the mortar.

Much of the Pennsylvania progression in building was repeated in

Ontario, although there is no evidence to indicate that even the earliest settlers resorted to cave dwellings. When the Mennonites arrived in Upper Canada, they made their first crude homes from logs in the same styles they had first used in Pennsylvania. Log houses became fairly elaborate in Waterloo and sometimes had a cantilevered second storey forebay overhanging the front of the house.[2] Plain stone houses with some Georgian influence were soon popular in Waterloo, where they were built of locally quarried stone in the familiar Germanic rectangle. Most had a fairly steeply pitched roof (often high enough to accommodate a two-storey attic) and sometimes a verandah supported by columns on the front or back of the house. In spite of the fact that the government levied a tax on every fireplace and stove, many of the stone houses boasted a combination of the two chimney styles, with a central chimney as well as one at each gable end.[3]

Mennonites in York County began to replace the log structures with permanent homes in the mid-nineteenth century, two or three generations after the initial period of settlement. By this time styles in homes, like furniture, had lost many of the Pennsylvania characteristics, although Georgian traits were found in most parts of the province long after they had been replaced by neo-classical styles in America. Even in Vaughan Township, where furniture-making remained close to its American roots, permanent homes were constructed in styles often different from the rural Pennsylvania traditions. This was due to the fact that architectural styles from surrounding communities crept in to season the plain American styles.

By mid-century the architecture surrounding the York County Mennonites offered a cornucopia of delights from which to choose. Alan Gowans, in his *Building Canada* describes Toronto as a "middle-class city . . . maintaining no historical pose. It was from the first freer to be up-to-date than other Canadian cities."[4] The latest styles in building came from England, then a supremely confident world power. In the British Isles, leaders of fashion borrowed from antiquity, and those within the sphere of influence of Toronto tended to be affected by such taste. Classical English styles were emulated in Toronto university buildings, private clubs, banks and in the large homes of the wealthier citizens.

York County Mennonites were no exception. Although stone houses were built in the basic rectangular Germanic mode, it was not uncommon for them to include elements of the picturesque, the Gothic or the Italianate. Roofs lost some of their steepness and frequently had one large gable over the door, sometimes with a Gothic window. Gables in the classical Greek fashion were added, and windows became larger as larger panes of glass became more commonly available. In some York County homes it is not uncommon to find the larger panes in lower windows and the small ones in upper windows. Verandahs, sometimes around two or three sides of the house, became as popular with Mennonites in York County as they were throughout the province at this time. And, as with all domestic architecture, especially in rural areas, local builders interpreted the styles they executed loosely; they had their own ideas of what a particular style should look like and often combined styles from more than one period in a single building.[5]

Attitudes towards building materials changed, and what had once been considered the most desirable medium in Pennsylvania was replaced by others thought to be both more attractive and more efficient. For instance, frame houses were thought to be both more tasteful and warmer than stone houses. Those stone houses which were built were often plastered over as they had been in Pennsylvania to keep out dampness, although the pastel colours that appeared on some Pennsylvania homes are not found in York County.

In some places brick was considered a more desirable material than stone, and bricks were made on the property where building was in progress until transportation from the brick yards in Toronto became feasible. Bricks made from local clay were usually salmon pink or red, but buff-coloured ones for quoin corners, a style that had been popular in early Pennsylvania dwellings, could be made from lighter coloured clays. In Markham, brick work sometimes was done by a non-Mennonite bricklayer, and the rest of the dwelling was completed by the Mennonite carpenter-owner.

Some frame houses had a construction unique to Markham. This consisted of a vertical siding of relatively narrow boards with a grooved joining. The seal on the V-groove was sufficiently tight that battens were unnecessary. In later years, when local mills began to use smaller timber, the siding boards became even narrower. The board and batten siding that had become generally popular by the 1850s was also used by the Mennonites on their homes, as was horizontal siding, which was also found on out-buildings.

One feature of Mennonite architecture which distinguished Mennonite homes from those of other settlers was the "grossdoddy" (German for grandfather) or "doddy" house. This practice of attaching a wing to the main house may have derived from the Pennsylvania tradition of building new, large homes onto existing smaller ones. In some cases the doddy house was the older, original part of the house; in others it was a newer, smaller addition.

In every Mennonite family older sons were set up on farms of their own. When the youngest son married, he inherited the family farm and took over the main house, while his aging parents moved into the doddy house. Some doddy houses were only one storey high, with bedroom, sitting room and kitchen all on one floor; others had a floor plan similar to that of the main house and rose two storeys with attic space above. In the latter plan the kitchen and sitting rooms would be on the first floor and the bedrooms on the upper floor. Sometimes both floors were connected with the main house. Although the doddy house was usually a completely self-contained unit, if space was limited it might be built without a kitchen, and its occupants would eat their meals with their children in the main house.

This kind of humane housing arrangement encouraged the older couple to be as independent as health allowed and as involved with the family as they chose. It also ensured that there was more than one adult male to help with the work of the farm and more than one adult female to share the work of the garden and to help with such activities as the fall canning. The doddy house was, then, the architectural manifestation of the Mennonite communal way of life. It was perhaps the most significant factor in the success of this lifestyle, enabling generations to live together comfortably and profitably.

In York County it is common to see these doddy houses, which were constructed a generation or even two after the main house, built in a different type of material and incorporating features of a later architectural style. The main house might, for instance, have been built with chimneys at the gable ends, while the doddy house had a centrally placed one. Some of the homes in the county have yet another wing on a side of the house, providing a residence for an unmarried sister or aunt. These additional "doddy" houses may have been constructed in yet a third type of material and in an even later architectural style.

Both the elevation and the set-back of the doddy house differed from that of the main house. Usually the front edge of the doddy house met the front edge of the verandah of the main house, and both units had a doorway onto this shared verandah as well as their own separate side or rear doors from the kitchen. The interior doorways between the main and doddy houses usually were formed by enlarging a window in the main house.

One of the most spectacular features of Mennonite homes, and a tradition that was brought from Pennsylvania, is the woodwork treatment in both the main and doddy houses. All of this woodwork — foot-high baseboards, broad door jambs and doors, the window framing and transoms — was paint-grained, often in imitation of the favourite bird's-eye maple commonly duplicated in the furniture. The effect, especially on a day when the sun is streaming through the windows, can be breathtaking.

Outside the typical Mennonite farm home were a number of outbuildings, the most important of which is still the barn. Recognizing that the success of their farms was linked with the well-being of their livestock, the Mennonites often built their barns thirty or forty years before they built their permanent homes. In Pennsylvania the barn was built into a hillside, with the livestock housed in the lower section. Building into a hill helped to moderate the temperature for the animals in hot weather and in cold, and it also made for easier access to the upper storey, since a ramp could be built up to the loft on the side where the lower storey was below ground. In Upper Canada barns were built this way but often on flat ground with a man-made ramp to the second storey. Some of the early barns in Vaughan were built with a cantilevered upper section, providing a sheltered area where the animals could loaf protected from the sun and rain. This sensible structure was adopted by settlers of many backgrounds.

Barns in Pennsylvania were often decorated with painted folk art symbols. The custom, which first originated in Europe, was first used on wooden homes and later transferred to the barn when stone houses replaced wooden structures. Folk art paintings did not become common in Pennsylvania until after 1830, however, and seem never to have appeared in York County. Instead, the Mennonites in this area left their barns unpainted, allowing the wood to age, and this became in effect a folk tradition among York County Mennonites.

Many York County Mennonite barns still have their unique, original wooden handles and hardware, and some still house the early aids to farming. One barn in Markham contains a wooden rack lift, an apparatus made of ratchets and ropes used to lift the wagon to the upper floor.

In addition to the barns, all Mennonite farms had a variety of other out-buildings, most of which were adapted from European or Pennsylvania prototypes. Often one of these out-buildings, probably the summer kitchen, would have been the original log home built by the first generation of settlers. Summer kitchens originated in North America, where extreme temperatures in the summer and large numbers of people at meals made them a necessity. These kitchens contained every implement essential for cooking and preparing meals, tubs and buckets for doing washing, plenty of storage space, a stove or fireplace and often a table and chairs where meals could be served to a small group.

The smokehouse was another common feature of the Mennonite farm. Here the Mennonites made the smoked sausages and meats of which they were so fond. The smokehouse was a small, windowless building, sometimes of squared log construction. In Pennsylvania, many Mennonite farms also had drying houses for drying fruits and vegetables to be used over the winter. The only drying houses found to date in York County are small movable units that were stored in the barn during the winter and taken outside to be used in the summer. They consisted of a number of shallow pull-out shelves of screening material on which the fruit was laid in single layers to dry.

The workshop was an extremely important part of the farm. It was the place where furniture was constructed, tools made or repaired, farm implements fashioned and even shoes made. The workshop was often equipped with a lathe and any other tools and materials necessary for the smooth operation of the farm. Usually a sizeable building, it often had more than one storey and numerous windows that provided ample light for working. In Pennsylvania many workshops also accommodated a smithy, but in York County separate structures were usually used for the two functions.

The history of Mennonite meeting houses is as long and as troubled as the history of the Anabaptist faith. The first meeting places originated in Switzerland. Forbidden by law, religious services had to be kept secret and so were incorporated into the homes of some of the members. The lower floor of the house was the "meeting house," while the upper storey served as living quarters for the family.[6] Many of the early meeting houses in Pennsylvania had this combination of church area and living quarters, with the bishop's or the minister's quarters under the same roof as the church. Meeting houses were built early in the history of the Pennsylvania settlement; the first one was built in Germantown in 1708. These early places of worship were plain log or stone structures furnished with backless benches. Later, when the living quarters ceased to occupy part of the building, they gained many embellishments. Some American Mennonite churches have Gothic doors and windows, soaring steeples and elaborate interiors.

In York County the first meeting houses were usually built by the first generation of settlers. These simple buildings were used only for religious services, since ceremonies such as weddings took place in the home. The Brethren in Christ congregation, however, met in each other's homes until 1877, when their first church was built. Although York County meeting houses appear not to have included living quarters, they nevertheless had more than one function; they served as church on Sunday and doubled as a school on week days. Often they were shared by more than one denomination. The Reesor Church on Steeles Avenue, for instance, was used by Mennonites on Sunday mornings and by the Presbyterian congregation on Sunday afternoons.

The typical meeting house was a simple rectangular structure built over a shallow foundation with no usable basement space. There were two doors at the front of the building (which never faced north), one slightly off-centre between two pairs of windows and one to the side of the front. Men and women entered through separate doors and sat on separate sides of the church, according to the arrangement of the synagogue as it was described in the Bible. This arrangement was also common in Quaker meeting houses. One Quaker meeting house in Newmarket, in the north part of the county, had sliding panels so that the women could be separated from the men during business meetings, but allowed to join them for worship.

Both the exterior and the interior of the Mennonite meeting houses were simple in construction. None had the elaborate verandahs, porches, towers or steeples found on the churches of other denominations. Like most other churches in the province, however, Mennonite meeting houses all had buggy sheds. These sheds remained in use longer in Mennonite churches, and some of the Mennonite churches in York County have preserved the original structures.

One of the few changes made to the buildings over the years was the addition of a basement, something deemed necessary when Sunday schools were established. Some meeting houses were completely rebuilt when basements were dug, making it difficult for historians to determine the nature of the early structures.

However a number of fine examples of early church construction still can be found in York County. One of the oldest, the Edgeley Mennonite Church, was built in Vaughan Township in 1824 on property that had been donated by Mennonite John Smith in 1801. The cemetery on the property was in use for many years before the meeting house was built, and simple field stones were at first used to mark gravesites. The earliest marked stone belongs to Henry Smith who died in 1823.

The Edgeley Church, which has recently been moved to Black Creek Pioneer Village, across the street from Vaughan Township on Steeles Avenue, looks much as it did when it was first erected. The original logs were up to one and a half feet thick and were held together by hand-forged nails. In 1848 they were covered with horizontal framing at a cost of $220, and the inside walls were sheathed in wide sheets of hand-planed cedar that shine like satin. The original furnishings are still in the church, including benches that cost $15 at the time and the wood stove that was added at a later date. This stove is of a distinctive construction; the top holds the sides together, and if it is lifted up, the sides of the stove fall to the ground. A small anteroom to one side in the church which contained cradles where infants were kept during the services now acts as storage space for firewood and burial tools. The roof of the structure, which has since been replaced, was of two-foot long shingles made from pine boards hand-shaved with a drawing knife.

The Cober Church, which also doubled as a school, was another early building in Vaughan Township. It was built by the Brethren in Christ congregation and later sold to the Dunkards. It still stands on its original location, one concession to the east of the Edgeley Church. The Cober Church is similar in construction to the Edgeley Church, but its outer siding is painted white. It is now privately owned and maintained.

The earliest Mennonite meeting house in York County was built by the Wideman congregation, and services were conducted in Dutch. Erected in 1816, the original log structure has since been replaced by an entirely new building of red brick with a full basement underneath. The double cradle that was once in use in this church (now in the Markham Museum), may have been made originally for the twins of one of the member families. One of the old pews, now also in the museum, indicates that the Wideman Church may not have been as austere in design and furnishings as other Mennonite meeting houses. The pew has the elaborately shaped legs and arms of the later Pennsylvania style.

Built in 1820, the Reesor Church in Markham is another fine example of Mennonite architecture. The church building has undergone a number of changes over the years; when a basement was built, the whole structure was turned to face east rather than south, and in 1857 the original log building was replaced by a frame one. But despite these changes, it still has separate entrances for men and women and separate seating sections on each side of a central aisle. A new church in the hamlet of Cedar Grove in Markham was built some years after the Reesor Church, when a number of members of the Reesor congregation split off and formed their own congregation.

All of these plain, still basically Germanic meeting houses share a simplicity and absence of decoration that gives them a quiet grandeur. The unadorned buildings, which remained true to the style of the old meeting houses of Pennsylvania and even Europe, seem to be a reaffirmation of a belief in a simple kind of life. Important enough to have been built very early in the history of each community, they remain a testament to that simple life.

Smoke houses were once a common feature of every German-Ontario farm. This one, on a Dunkard farm in Vaughan, is one of the few that remain. It has a tin roof and is constructed of squared logs.

(Top) Board and batten siding was becoming a popular building material during the mid-nineteenth century when many Mennonite farm homes were built. This house shows other features also coming into vogue at that time. The doddy house at the right is of V-groove siding.

The original log structure of the Reesor Mennonite Church in Markham was built in 1820 and faced south. A frame building replaced it in 1857 or 1858. Later the church was raised so that a basement could be added, and the building was turned to face east. The buggy shed, once common outside many churches, still stands beside the church.

This Markham Mennonite farm home shows the V-groove siding frequently used in the township. Built in 1878, it has a verandah and private entrance, while the doddy house on the far side of the building has its own completely separate entrance.

(Top) Edgeley Mennonite Church, now in Black Creek Pioneer Village, was built in Vaughan in 1824 of squared, horizontal-dressed logs (some more than a foot and a half thick). In 1848 the exterior was sheathed with unpainted frame siding. The door and window placement are typical of Mennonite meeting houses, as is the centrally-located chimney. The original hand-shaved shingle roof was replaced some years ago.

Summer kitchens were an important feature of early farmsteads. On this Dunkard farm both the main and the doddy house had their own summer kitchens, both of them two storeys high. In the one on the right, the lower windows have large panes of glass while the upper-storey windows have smaller ones. Both kitchens are of unpainted frame.

(Top) This brick house was built in 1836 and the two doddy houses were added at a later date. The two doddy houses are very different in style from the main house. Note the symmetrical door and window placement and the gable-end chimneys.

This stone farm house, the original Barkey family home, was built on property acquired in 1810. The main part of the house has gable-end chimneys, classical gables, symmetrical fenestration and a small circular window above the front door, as well as a roof that has lost much of the steep pitch that distinguished stone houses in Pennsylvania. The doddy house is the wing at the left.

Paint-grained woodwork was a feature of many Pennsylvania homes and later appeared in Upper Canada. These door frames and baseboards in a doddy house in Markham are of pine and have been painted to simulate bird's-eye maple.

Conclusion

The Mennonite community in York County leads a Damoclean existence today. Most of the Vaughan settlement has already been disrupted by the railways, and Markham is imperilled from two quarters — from Metropolitan Toronto with its voracious appetite for land and from the proposed airport that has necessitated expropriations. Many of the old families are now leaving the county and moving to farm districts more remote from urban centres.

It is therefore urgent to record the pioneer past before all evidence of it vanishes. Much of the German-Ontario tradition has been ignored in past decades, and it is only lately it has begun to be re-appraised and its contribution to the settlement of the province appreciated.

Lately the Anabaptists themselves have begun to reassess their past. It has given them new pride in their heritage to know, for instance, that the Mennonite Central Relief Committee was the model for John F. Kennedy's Peace Corps in the United States. And despite a history of internal dissention, a newly awakened consciousness of a common background has brought them together to preserve the old traditions and beliefs for the future.

With the current emphasis on older, homelier ways of doing things, the crafts of the Mennonites, most notably quilt-making and woodworking (although on a much smaller scale than previously), are enjoying a renewed popularity. Craft fairs are more and more strongly attended every year.

But the Mennonite way of life has been, to a certain extent, as much a victim of progress as of airports and railways. Old-age homes are a new feature in the Mennonite community, and doddy houses may soon be a thing of the past. The current exodus to new farm areas will mean that the furniture will be taken away from the setting that identified it. A tradition is coming to an end.

But Mennonites, as they have demonstrated for centuries, are survivors. They will put down new roots, build new homes and construct new churches. Their stay in the new places will again be recorded by the little things of daily life rather than great monuments.

A new tradition is beginning.

Notes

Chapter 1 Dissent and Exodus

1. See Frank Epp, *Mennonites in Canada: The History of a Separate People*, p. 29.
2. Cited in *Mennonites in Canada*, p. 23.
3. *Mennonites in Canada*, p. 30.
4. For a discussion of the development of Anabaptism, see Harold S. Bender and C. Henry Smith, eds, *The Mennonite Encyclopedia*, vol. 2, p. 304.
5. For a concise review of changes in construction techniques, see Edward Joy, *Furniture* (London: The Connoisseur, 1972), p. 14.
6. A description of the founding of this settlement appears in *The Mennonite Encyclopedia*, vol. 2, p. 136.
7. For a discussion of Mennonite farming techniques, see *Ibid.*, vol. 2, p. 308.
8. A description of Pennsylvania German dwellings appears in Irwin Richman, *Pennsylvania Architecture*, pp. 1-6.
9. See Amos Long Jr., *The Pennsylvania German Family Farm*, vol. 4, p. 7.
10. See Jean Lipman, *American Folk Art Decoration*, p. 11.
11. For a discussion of early chair construction, see Joseph T. Butler, *American Furniture*, p. 11.
12. See *Mennonites in Canada*, pp. 51-52 for a description of the change in attitude towards the Mennonites at this time.

Chapter 2 The Journey to Upper Canada

1. Vol. 1, p. 150.
2. For a comprehensive treatment of the opening of Upper Canada to settlement, see Lillian Gates, *Land Policies of Upper Canada*.
3. An excellent account of the first Mennonite settlers and their journey appears in Epp, *Mennonites in Canada*, pp. 56-57.

4. *Ibid.*, p. 68.
5. For a discussion of Mennonite customs and traditions see Blodwen Davies, "Mennonite Folklore in Ontario", 1958 Report, Archives of Ontario, Miscellaneous Collection, No. 4, Acc. No. 2941.
6. "The History of Markham".

Chapter 3 The Furniture and Its Makers

1. We are indebted to John MacIntyre for much of this information on the Quakers and John Doan. His research has done much to preserve the history of these people.
2. See Ann Crawford, ed., *Henry Snider: His Ancestors and Descendants*, for a more complete discussion of the Snider furniture-makers.
3. *Ibid.*, p. 1.
4. This information is contained in unpublished material compiled by John MacIntyre.
5. July, 1856.

Chapter 4 The Homes and Meeting Houses

1. The sources for the following discussion of early Pennsylvania Mennonite architecture are: Amos Long, Jr., *The Pennsylvania German Family Farm*; Frederic Klees, *The Pennsylvania Dutch*; Irwin Richman, *Pennsylvania Architecture*; J.J. Stoudt, *Early Pennsylvania Arts and Crafts*; Bender and Smith, *The Mennonite Encyclopedia*, vol. 1.
2. See, for example, Alan Gowans, *Building Canada: An Architectural History of Canadian Life*, plate 4.
3. *Ibid.*, plate 45.
4. p. 81.
5. For a complete discussion of rural Ontario architecture touching on Mennonite architecture, see V.S. Blake and R. Greenhill, *Rural Ontario*.
6. A brief discussion of meeting houses appears in "The York Pioneer and Historical Society Report for 1946", Archives of Ontario, and in Marion MacRae and Anthony Adamson, *Hallowed Walls*, pp. 182-3. We are indebted to Douglas Richardson for his advice on this chapter.

Bibliography

The Mennonites

Bender, Harold S. and C. Henry Smith, eds. *The Mennonite Encyclopedia*. Scottdale, Pa: The Mennonite Publishing House, 1955, 1969.

Crawford, Ann, ed. *Henry Snider: His Ancestors and Descendants*. Vaughan Township: The Snider Genealogical and Historical Research Group, 1976.

Epp, Frank H. *Mennonites in Canada: The History of a Separate People*. Toronto: Macmillan of Canada, 1974.

Fretz, J. Winfield. *The Mennonites in Ontario*. Waterloo: The Mennonite Historical Society of Ontario, 1974.

Klees, Frederic. *The Pennsylvania Dutch*. New York: Macmillan, 1951.

The Reesor Family in Canada: A Trail Through the Centuries, 1804-1950. Introduction by Blodwen Davies. Markham Township: Genealogical and Historical Records, 1950.

Upper Canada

Gates, Lillian. *Land Policies of Upper Canada*. Toronto: University of Toronto Press, 1968.

Gourlay, Robert. *A Statistical Account of Upper Canada*. New York: Johnson Reprint Corp., 1966.

"Historical Sketch of Markham Township: 1793-1950". Markham Township: The Markham Historical Committee.

"The History of Markham". Markham Township: Markham Public Library Archives.

Mitchell, John. *The Settlement of York County*. County of York: The Municipal Corporation, 1950.

Reaman, G. Elmore. *The Trail of the Black Walnut*. Toronto: McClelland and

Stewart, 1957, 1974.

—————————. *A History of Vaughan Township: Two centuries of life in the township.* Vaughan Township: Vaughan Historical Society, 1971.

Wood, J. David. ed. *Perspectives on Landscape and Settlement in Nineteenth Century Ontario.* Toronto: McClelland and Stewart, 1975.

Furniture

Boger, Louise Ada. *The Complete Guide to Furniture Styles.* New York: Charles Scribner's Sons, 1959.

—————————. *Furniture Past and Present.* New York: Doubleday, 1966.

Butler, Joseph T. *American Furniture.* London: Triune Books, 1973.

Dobson, Henry and Barbara. *The Early Furniture of Ontario and the Atlantic Provinces.* Toronto: M.F. Feheley Publishers, 1974.

The Encyclopedia of Antiques. London: Phoebus Publishing in co-operation with Octopus Books, 1976.

Gamon, Albert. *Pennsylvania Country Antiques.* New Jersey: Prentice-Hall, 1968.

Joy, Edward, *Furniture.* London: The Connoisseur, 1972.

McMurray, A. Lynn. "Ontario-German Decorative Arts", in Donald Webster, ed. *The Book of Canadian Antiques.* Toronto: McGraw-Hill Ryerson, 1974.

Shackleton, Philip. *The Furniture of Old Ontario.* Toronto: Macmillan, 1973.

Singleton, Esther. *Dutch and Flemish Furniture.* New York: McClure, 1907.

Wanscher, Ole. *The Art of Furniture: 5,000 Years of Furniture and Interiors.* New York: Reinhold, 1966.

Decoration

Good, E. Reginald. *Anna's Art.* Kitchener: Pochauna Publications, 1976.

Lipman, Jean. *American Folk Decoration.* New York: Oxford University Press, 1951.

Lipman, Jean and Alice Winchester. *The Flowering of American Folk Art.* New York: Viking Press in co-operation with the Whitney Museum of American Art, 1974.

Stoudt, J. J. *Early Pennsylvania Arts and Crafts.* New York: A.S. Barnes, 1964.

Architecture

Arthur, Eric and Dudley Witney. *Barns.* Toronto: McClelland and Stewart, 1972.

Blake, Verschoyle Benson and Ralph Greenhill. *Rural Ontario.* Toronto: University of Toronto Press, 1969.

Gowans, Alan. *Building Canada: An Architectural History of Canadian Life.* Toronto: Oxford University Press, 1966.

Greenhill, R., K. MacPherson and D. Richardson. *Ontario Towns.* Ottawa: Oberon Press, 1974.

Long, Amos Jr. *The Pennsylvania German Family Farm.* Breinigsville, Pa: The Pennsylvania German Society, 1972.

MacRae, Marion and Anthony Adamson. *Hallowed Walls: Church Architecture of Upper Canada.* Toronto: Clarke Irwin, 1975.

Pennsylvania German Barns. Allentown, Pa: The Pennsylvania German Folklore Society, 1956.

Ritchie, T. *Canada Builds.* Toronto: University of Toronto Press, 1967.

Richman, Irwin. *Pennsylvania's Architecture.* Pennsylvania Historical Studies No. 10. University Park, Pa: The Pennsylvania Historical Association, 1969.